STEP-BY-STEP

Recipes with Yogurt

Recipes with Yogurt

PAMELA WESTLAND

SHOOTING STAR PRESS

This edition printed in 1995 for:
Shooting Star Press Inc
230 Fifth Avenue – Suite 1212
New York, NY 10001

Shooting Star Press books are available at special discounts for bulk purchases for sales promotions, premiums, fund-raising, or educational use. Special edition or book excerpts can also be created to specification. For details contact: Special Sales Director, Shooting Star Press Inc., 230 Fifth Avenue, Suite 1212, New York, NY 10001

ISBN 1 56924 184 8

Printed in Italy

Acknowledgements:

Design & DTP: Pedro & Frances Prá-Lopez / Kingfisher Design
Art Direction: Pedro Prá-Lopez
Managing Editor: Alexa Stace
Special Photography: Amanda Heywood
Home Economist: Louise Pickford
Stylist: Marion Price
Photograph page 75: Clive Streeter
Step-by-step Photographs page 74: Karl Adamson

Gas Hob supplied by New World Domestic Appliances Ltd
Photographs on pages 6, 14, 26, 34 & 54: By courtesy of ZEFA

Note:
All eggs are medium unless otherwise stated

Contents

FIRST COURSES   *page* 7

Artichoke Mousse 9
Smoked Salmon Cheesecake..................10
Yogurt & Spinach Soup 12

FISH   *page* 15

Poached Salmon 16
Quenelles & Watercress Sauce..............18
Baked Red Snapper 20
Fish & Seafood Chowder 22
Shrimp Curry & Fruit Sauce 25

VEGETABLES   *page* 27

Cauliflower Roulade 28
Vegetable Medley 31
Spinach Pancakes..................................32

MEAT & POULTRY   *page* 35

Crispy-coated Baby Chicken 36
Lamb Kebabs & Cucumber Sauce 38
Moussaka 40
Orchard Pork 42
Ham & Chicken Pie 44

Tandoori Chicken 47
Spicy Meatballs....................................48
Roast Leg of Lamb 51
Rabbit with Fried Cheese 52

DESSERTS & CAKES   *page* 55

Apricot Brûlée......................................56
Chocolate Chip Ice Cream..................58
Pashka 61
Boston Chocolate Pie 62
Cherry Clafoutis..................................64
Yogurt Muffins....................................66
Truffle Cheesecake..............................68
Danish Lemon Cake 71
Scottish Gingerbread 72
Passion Cake 74

WHAT IS YOGURT?   *page* 76

Making Yogurt......................................76
Yogurt Cheese......................................77
Yogurt Drinks......................................78
Flavoring Yogurt 79

Index..80

First Courses

Yogurt has a delicious contribution to make in a wide range
of first courses. You can use it in place of cream in mousses
and cheesecakes, to complement flavors as diverse as those of
Jerusalem artichokes and smoked salmon. You can combine
yogurt with light chicken stock and beaten eggs
to make a Middle-Eastern-style soup, or garnish a wide range
of creamy vegetable or fish soups with a swirl of yogurt.

You can also serve a selection of yogurt salads as a first course with
style, offering, for example, avocado sauce and cucumber
salad with potato chips and crackers, breadsticks and fresh
vegetable crudités. Or you can toss mixed leaf and vegetable salads
with a piquant yogurt and lemon or vinaigrette dressing.
In contrast, try serving melt-in-the-mouth fried yogurt cheese
(from the recipe on page 77) with a small side salad
and plenty of warm, crusty bread.

*Opposite: Healthy drinks and
snacks are quick and easy to
whip up with yogurt, and
assorted fruits and nuts.*

ARTICHOKE MOUSSE

Artichoke hearts have a characteristic tanginess, well complemented by a colorful bell pepper salad in this stylish first course.

STEP 2

SERVES 6

15 oz can artichoke hearts
²/₃ cup condensed consommé
juice of ¹/₂ orange
large pinch of grated nutmeg
4 tbsp warm water
1 envelope gelatine
2 egg whites
1¹/₄ cups thick-set yogurt
salt and pepper

SALAD:
3 large bell peppers, various colors
3 tbsp olive oil
juice of ¹/₂ orange
2 tbsp natural yogurt
2 tbsp chopped parsley

1 Drain the artichoke hearts, and reserve the liquid. Place the hearts in a food processor with 3 tablespoons of liquid, the consommé, orange juice, and nutmeg. Process until finely chopped but not puréed. Season, pour into a large bowl and set aside.

2 Pour the water into a small bowl and sprinkle on the gelatine. Place the bowl in a pan of simmering water and stir until the crystals have dissolved, then remove and set aside to cool.

3 Whisk the egg whites until they are stiff but not dry.

4 When the gelatine is syrupy and on the point of setting, blend well into the artichoke mixture. Stir in the yogurt, using an up-and-over movement, until thoroughly blended. Fold in the egg whites, using a metal spoon. Pour into a wetted ring mold or 6 individual molds, cover and chill for at least 3 hours or until set.

5 Heat the broiler to high and sear the bell peppers close to the heat until evenly blackened all over. Plunge into cold water and as soon as they are cool enough to handle peel off the skins. Core and seed, cut into thick strips, and leave to cool.

6 Beat together the olive oil, orange juice, and yogurt and season. Pour over the bell peppers and stir in the chopped parsley.

7 Run a knife around the inside of the molds and invert onto serving plates, shaking the mold to release it. Pile the salad into the center of the mold and serve chilled, with crispy rolls or black rye bread.

STEP 4

STEP 5

STEP 7

STEP 2a

STEP 2b

STEP 3

STEP 5

SMOKED SALMON CHEESECAKE

This rich, creamy cheesecake makes a memorable first course for a special occasion. You can also serve it as a lunch or supper dish,

SERVES 6

6 tbsp butter
2¹/₃ cups unsalted white crackers, crushed
1 tbsp sesame seeds
salt and pepper

FILLING:
6 oz smoked salmon pieces, roughly chopped
grated rind and juice of 1 lemon
1 cup full fat soft cheese
2 eggs, separated
²/₃ cup natural yogurt
freshly ground black pepper
4 tbsp warm water
1 envelope gelatine

TOPPING:
²/₃ cup thick-set yogurt
4 thin slices lemon
a few sprigs of fresh dill
12 whole shrimp (optional)

1 Grease an 8-in spring-form cake pan.

2 Melt the butter in a saucepan. Remove from the heat, stir in the cracker crumbs and sesame seeds and season. Press the mixture evenly over the base of the prepared pan and chill.

3 Process the smoked salmon and lemon juice briefly in a food processor, then turn into a bowl and beat in the cheese, egg yolks, and yogurt. Season well with pepper.

4 Pour the water into a small bowl and sprinkle on the gelatine. Place the bowl in a saucepan of simmering water and stir until the crystals have dissolved. Remove from heat, set aside to cool. When the gelatine is syrupy and on the point of setting, pour into the salmon mixture and stir to blend thoroughly.

5 Whisk the egg whites until stiff but not dry. Using a metal spoon, fold them into the fish mixture until they are well blended. Pour the filling into the prepared pan and level the surface. Chill for 3-4 hours until set.

6 Lift the cheesecake out of the pan, keeping it on the metal base, and place on a flat serving dish. Spread the yogurt evenly over the top or place in a pastry bag and pipe swirls. Cut the lemon slices in quarters and arrange in pairs to form butterfly shapes around the rim of the cheesecake. Arrange the dill sprigs on top and garnish with the shrimp, if using. Serve chilled.

STEP 1

STEP 3

STEP 4

STEP 5

YOGURT & SPINACH SOUP

Whole young spinach leaves add vibrant color to this unusual soup.

SERVES 4

2¹/₂ cups chicken stock
4 tbsp long-grain rice, rinsed and drained
4 tbsp water
1 tbsp cornstarch
2¹/₂ cups natural yogurt
juice of 1 lemon
3 egg yolks, lightly beaten
9 cups young spinach leaves, washed and
   drained
salt and pepper

1 Pour the stock into a large saucepan, season, and bring to the boil. Add the rice and simmer for 10 minutes, until barely cooked. Remove from the heat.

2 Pour the water into a small bowl and sift the cornstarch into it. Stir to make a thin, smooth paste.

3 Pour the yogurt into a second saucepan and stir in the cornstarch mixture. Set the pan over a low heat and bring the yogurt slowly to the boil, stirring with a wooden spoon in one direction only. This will stabilize the yogurt and prevent it from separating or curdling on contact with the hot stock. When the yogurt has reached boiling point, turn the heat down and simmer slowly for 10 minutes. Remove from the heat and allow the mixture to cool slightly before stirring in the beaten egg yolks.

4 Pour the yogurt mixture into the stock, stir in the lemon juice, and stir to blend thoroughly. Keep the soup warm, but do not allow it to boil.

5 Blanch the spinach leaves in boiling, salted water for 2-3 minutes until they begin to soften but have not collapsed. Tip the spinach into a colander, drain well and stir it into the soup. Taste the soup and adjust the seasoning if necesary. Serve in wide shallow soup plates, with hot, crusty bread.

TO STABILIZE YOGURT

When stabilizing yogurt in the way described, it is important to stir it slowly and rhythmically in one direction only. Do not cover the pan, because any drops of condensation falling into the yogurt could cause it to separate. And do not be tempted to swish it about in first one direction and then the other.

CHAPTER TWO

Fish

Yogurt has a subtle and sometimes undetected part to play
in fish dishes of all kinds. In the dish of Baked Red Snapper,
for example (page 20), which has the aroma and flavor
of Greek island cookery, it is yogurt that harmonizes
the fragrances and flavors of the herbs,
garlic, and vegetables.

And in the accompanying salad, it is yogurt that neutralizes
any sharpness there may be in fresh vegetable leaves.
Yogurt also plays a key role in smooth tangy dishes,
such as Shrimp Curry & Fruit Sauce (page 25), and
gives a new slant on poaching salmon steaks.
In fact, yogurt is the perfect partner for fish –
try the Fish & Seafood Chowder on page 22
and taste the difference.

Opposite: *A Sicilian fisherman mends his nets in the port of Palermo. Yogurt makes a very good partner for fish of all kinds, providing the basis for smooth, subtly-flavored sauces.*

STEP 1

STEP 2

STEP 3

STEP 4

POACHED SALMON

Salmon steaks, poached in a well-flavored stock and served with a piquant sauce, make a delicious summer lunch or supper dish.

SERVES 4

1 small onion, sliced
1 small carrot, sliced
1 stick celery, sliced
1 bay leaf
pared rind and juice of ½ orange
a few stalks of parsley
salt
5-6 black peppercorns
3 cups water
4 salmon steaks, about 12 oz each
salad leaves, to serve
lemon twists, to garnish

SAUCE:

1 large avocado, peeled, halved and stoned
½ cup thick-set yogurt
grated rind and juice of ½ orange
black pepper
a few drops of hot red pepper sauce

1 Put the onion, carrot, celery, bay leaf, orange rind, orange juice, parsley stalks, salt, and peppercorns in a saucepan just large enough to take the salmon steaks in a single layer. Pour on the water, cover, and bring to the boil. Simmer the stock for 20 minutes.

2 Arrange the salmon steaks in the saucepan, return the stock to the boil, and simmer for 3 minutes. Cover, remove from the heat and leave the salmon to cool in the stock.

3 To make the sauce, roughly chop the avocado and place it in a blender or food processor with the yogurt, orange rind and orange juice. Process to make a smooth sauce, then season to taste with salt, pepper, and hot pepper sauce.

4 Remove the salmon steaks from the stock (reserve it to make fish soup or a sauce), skin them, and pat dry with paper towels.

5 Cover the serving dish with salad leaves, arrange the salmon steaks on top and spoon a little of the sauce into the center of each one. Garnish the fish with lemon twists, and serve the remaining sauce separately.

ACCOMPANIMENT

The salmon could be served with New Potato Salad (see page 76) as an ideal accompaniment.

STEP 3

STEP 4a

STEP 4b

STEP 5

QUENELLES & WATERCRESS SAUCE

The quenelles, made from a thick purée of fish and yogurt, can be prepared well in advance and stored in the refrigerator.

SERVES 4

1½ lb white fish fillets, skinned
2 small egg whites
½ tsp ground cilantro
1 tsp ground mace
⅔ cup natural yogurt
1 small onion, sliced
salt and pepper
mixture of boiled Basmati rice and wild rice,
    to serve

SAUCE:
1 bunch watercress, trimmed
1¼ cups chicken stock
2 tbsp cornstarch
⅔ cup natural yogurt
2 tbsp crème fraîche

1 Cut the fish into pieces and process it in a food processor for about 30 seconds, until it is finely chopped.

2 Add the egg whites to the fish and process for a further 30 seconds until the mixture forms a stiff paste. Add the cilantro and mace and season. Add the yogurt and process until well blended. Transfer the mixture to a covered container and chill it for at least 30 minutes.

3 Spoon the mixture into a pastry bag, and pipe into sausage shapes about 4 in long. Cut off each length with a knife. Alternatively, take heaped tablespoons of the mixture and shape into ovals, using 2 spoons.

4 Bring about 2 in of water to the boil in a skillet and add the onion for flavoring. Lower the quenelles into the water, using a fish slice or spoon. Cover the pan, keep the water at a gentle rolling boil and poach the quenelles for 8 minutes, turning them once. Remove with a slotted spoon and drain on paper towels.

5 To make the sauce, roughly chop the watercress, reserving a few sprigs for garnish. Process the remainder with the chicken stock until well blended, then pour into a small saucepan. Stir the cornstarch into the yogurt and pour the mixture into the pot. Bring to the boil, stirring. Stir in the crème fraîche, season, and remove from the heat. Pour the sauce into a warmed dish and serve it separately.

6 Garnish with the reserved watercress sprigs. Serve with a Basmati rice and wild rice mixture.

STEP 1

STEP 2

STEP 4a

STEP 4b

BAKED RED SNAPPER

*You can substitute other whole fish for the snapper,
or use cutlets of cod or halibut.*

SERVES 4
OVEN: 375°F

1 red snapper, or other whole fish, about
    2 lb, cleaned
juice of 2 limes, or 1 lemon
4-5 sprigs of thyme, lemon thyme or
    parsley
3 tbsp olive oil
1 large onion, chopped
2 garlic cloves, finely chopped
1 x 14-oz can chopped tomatoes
2 tbsp tomato paste
2 tbsp red wine vinegar
5 tbsp thick-set yogurt
2 tbsp chopped parsley
2 tsp dried oregano
6 tbsp dry breadcrumbs
$\frac{1}{4}$ cup yogurt cheese (see page 77), or
    feta cheese, crumbled
salt and pepper
lime wedges and dill sprigs, to serve

SALAD:
1 small lettuce, thickly sliced
10-12 young spinach leaves, torn
$\frac{1}{2}$ small cucumber, sliced and quartered
4 scallions, thickly sliced
3 tbsp chopped parsley
2 tbsp olive oil
2 tbsp natural yogurt
1 tbsp red wine vinegar

1 Wash the fish and dry with paper
towels. Sprinkle the lime or lemon
juice inside and over the fish, and season
well. Place the herbs inside the fish.

2 Heat the oil in a saucepan and fry
the onion until translucent. Stir in
the garlic and cook for 1 minute, then
stir in the chopped tomatoes, tomato
paste and wine vinegar. Bring to the boil
and simmer, uncovered, for 5 minutes
until it has thickened slightly.

3 Remove from the heat, allow the
sauce to cool a little, then stir in the
yogurt, parsley, and oregano.

4 Pour half the sauce into a shallow,
ovenproof dish just large enough to
take the fish. Pour the remainder of the
sauce over it, and sprinkle on the
breadcrumbs. Bake uncovered for 30-35
minutes, until it is firm. Sprinkle the
yogurt cheese or feta over the fish and
serve with lime wedges and dill sprigs.
Serve the salad separately.

5 Arrange the lettuce, spinach,
cucumber, scallions, and parsley in
a bowl. Whisk the oil, yogurt, and wine
vinegar until well blended, and pour over
the salad.

STEP 1

STEP 2

STEP 3

STEP 4

FISH & SEAFOOD CHOWDER

Served with warm crusty bread and a salad, this tasty soup makes a substantial lunch or supper dish.

SERVES 4

3¹/₂ pints mussels in their shells
1 large onion, thinly sliced
2 garlic cloves, chopped
3 bay leaves
a few stalks of parsley
a few stalks of thyme
1¹/₄ cups water
¹/₂ lb smoked haddock fillets
1 lb potatoes, peeled and diced
4 celery stalks, thickly sliced
1 x 8-oz can corn kernels, drained and rinsed
²/₃ cup natural yogurt
1 tsp cornstarch
²/₃ cup dry white wine
¹/₂ tsp cayenne pepper, or to taste
black pepper
2 tbsp chopped parsley

1 Scrub the mussels, pull off the "beards", and rinse in several changes of cold water. Discard any open shells that remain open when tapped.

2 Put the onion, garlic, bay leaves, parsley, and thyme in a large saucepan and pour on the water. Add the mussels, cover, and cook over high heat for 5 minutes, shaking the pot once or twice.

3 Line a colander with muslin or cheesecloth and stand it in a bowl. Strain the mussel liquor into the bowl. Remove and shell the mussels and set them aside. Discard the vegetables and herbs and reserve the liquor.

4 Put the haddock, potatoes, and celery into the rinsed pan, add 2½ cups of cold water and bring to the boil. Cover the pan and simmer for 10 minutes. Remove the haddock with a fish slice and skin, bone and flake it. Remove the vegetables with a slotted spoon and strain the liquor into the reserved seafood liquor.

5 Return the cooking liquor to the rinsed saucepan, add the corn and bring to the boil. Stir together the yogurt and cornstarch to make a smooth paste. Stir in a little of the fish liquor, then pour it into the saucepan. Stir until the yogurt is well blended, then add the reserved mussels, haddock, potatoes, and celery. Add the white wine, season with cayenne and black pepper, and heat the soup gently, without boiling. Taste and adjust the seasoning if necessary. Transfer to a warm serving dish and sprinkle with the chopped parsley. Serve hot, with crusty bread.

SHRIMP CURRY & FRUIT SAUCE

Serve this lightly-spiced dish as part of a buffet meal, or as a
refreshingly different lunch dish, with rice.

SERVES 4
2 tbsp vegetable oil
2 tbsp butter
2 onions, finely chopped
2 garlic cloves, finely chopped
1 tsp cumin seeds, lightly crushed
1 tsp ground turmeric
1 tsp paprika
$^1/_2$ tsp chili powder, or to taste
$^1/_2$ cucumber, thinly diced
$^3/_4$- 1 cup shredded coconut
1 x 15-oz can chopped tomatoes
1 tbsp tomato paste
$2^3/_4$- 3 cups frozen shrimps, defrosted
$^2/_3$ cup thick-set yogurt
2 hard-boiled eggs, quartered
salt
cilantro leaves and onion rings, to garnish

FRUIT SAUCE:
$1^1/_4$ cups natural yogurt
$^1/_4$ tsp salt
1 garlic clove, crushed
2 tbsp chopped mint
4 tbsp seedless raisins
1 small pomegranate

1 Heat the oil and butter in a skillet. Add the chopped onions and fry until translucent. Add the garlic and fry for a further minute, until softened but not browned.

2 Stir in the cumin seeds, turmeric, paprika, and chili powder and cook for 2 minutes, stirring. Stir in the coconut, chopped tomatoes, and tomato paste and bring to the boil. Simmer for 10 minutes, or until the sauce has thickened slightly. It should not be at all runny.

3 Remove from the heat and set aside to cool. Stir in the shrimp, cucumber, and yogurt. Taste the sauce and adjust the seasoning if necessary. Cover and chill until ready to serve.

4 To make the fruit sauce, place the yogurt in a bowl and stir in the salt, garlic, mint, and raisins. Cut the pomegranate in half, scoop out the seeds and discard the white membrane. Stir the seeds into the yogurt, reserving a few for garnish.

5 Transfer the curry to a serving dish and arrange the hard-boiled egg, cilantro leaves, and onion rings on top. Serve the sauce separately, sprinkled with the reserved pomegranate seeds.

Vegetables

Yogurt is the perfect low-fat partner in vegetable dishes
of all kinds, from Spinach Pancakes with an interesting
filling (page 32) to an elegant Cauliflower Roulade (page 28),
and gives vegetarian dishes a satisfyingly piquant taste.

Yogurt cheese proves its versatility in this chapter, too,
as a satisfying homemade substitute for either cottage
cheese or low-fat soft cheese. If you do decide to
extend your repertoire and try your hand at simple
cheesemaking, you will find tasty ways to
use it to delicious advantage. See page 77 for easy
instructions on how to make this tasty cheese.

Opposite: *The crisp fresh leaves
of vegetables and salads blend
perfectly with yogurt to make
healthy, low-fat dishes.*

STEP 3

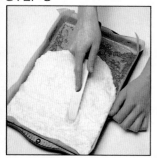

STEP 4

STEP 6

STEP 7

CAULIFLOWER ROULADE

A light-as-air mixture of eggs and vegetables produces a stylish vegetarian dish that can be enjoyed hot or cold.

SERVES 6
OVEN: 400°F

1 small cauliflower, divided into flowerets
4 eggs, separated
$^3/_4$ cup Cheddar, grated
$^1/_4$ cup yogurt cheese (see page 77), or
    cottage cheese
large pinch of grated nutmeg
$^1/_2$ tsp mustard powder
salt and pepper

FILLING:
1 bunch watercress, trimmed
$^1/_4$ cup butter
$^1/_4$ cup flour
$^3/_4$ cup natural yogurt
$^1/_4$ cup Cheddar, grated
$^1/_4$ cup yogurt cheese (see page 77), or
    cottage cheese

1 Line a 1-in deep baking sheet with parchment paper.

2 Steam the cauliflower until just tender. Drain and run cold water on it to prevent further cooking. Place the cauliflower in a food processor and chop finely.

3 Beat the egg yolks, then stir in the cauliflower, ½ cup of the Cheddar

and the yogurt cheese. Season with salt, nutmeg, mustard, and pepper. Whisk the egg whites until stiff but not dry, then fold into the cauliflower mixture, using a metal spoon.

4 Spread the mixture evenly in the prepared pan and bake in the preheated oven for 20-25 minutes, until well risen and golden brown.

5 Finely chop the watercress, reserving a few sprigs for garnish. Melt the butter in a small saucepan and add the watercress. Cook for 3 minutes, stirring, until it has collapsed. Blend in the flour, then the yogurt and simmer for 2 minutes. Stir in the cheeses.

6 Turn out the roulade onto a damp dish towel covered with parchment paper. Peel off the paper and leave 1 minute for the steam to escape. Roll up the roulade, with a new sheet of paper, starting from one narrow end.

7 Unroll the roulade, spread the filling to within 1 in of the edges, and roll up tightly. Place on a baking sheet, sprinkle on the remaining Cheddar and return to the oven for 5 minutes. Serve hot or cold.

VEGETABLE MEDLEY

Serve this as a crisp and colorful vegetarian dish, with pita bread,
or as an accompaniment to roast or broiled meats.

SERVES 4

1 cup young, tender green beans
8 baby carrots
6 baby turnips
½ small cauliflower
2 tbsp vegetable oil
2 large onions, sliced
2 garlic cloves, finely chopped
1¼ cups natural yogurt
1 tbsp cornstarch
2 tbsp tomato paste
large pinch of chili powder
salt

1 Cut the ends off the beans and snap them in half. Cut the carrots in half and the turnips in quarters. Divide the cauliflower into flowerets, discarding the thickest part of the stalk. Steam the vegetables over boiling water for 3 minutes, then turn them into a colander and plunge them at once in a large bowl of cold water to prevent further cooking.

2 Heat the oil in a saucepan and fry the onions until they are translucent. Stir in the garlic and cook for 1 further minute.

3 Mix together the yogurt, cornstarch and tomato paste to form a smooth paste. Stir this paste into the onions and cook for 1-2 minutes until the sauce is well blended.

4 Drain the vegetables well, then gradually stir them into the sauce, taking care not to break them up. Season with salt and chili powder to taste, cover and simmer gently for 5 minutes, until the vegetables are just tender. Taste and adjust the seasoning if necessary. Serve immediately.

STEP 1b

STEP 3

PITAS

You can serve this lightly-spiced vegetable dish as a filling for pita pockets. To do this, thicken the sauce slightly by simmering it, uncovered, before adding the partly-cooked vegetables. To make the snack more substantial, you can serve the filled pitas with sizzling sausages or wooden skewers of broiled lamb.

STEP 4

STEP 1

STEP 3

STEP 4

STEP 5

SPINACH PANCAKES

Serve these pancakes as a light lunch or supper dish, with tomato and basil salad for a dramatic color contrast.

SERVES 4
OVEN: 350°F

¾ cup wholewheat flour
1 egg
⅔ cup natural yogurt
3 tbsp water
1 tbsp vegetable oil, plus extra for brushing
2 cups frozen leaf spinach, defrosted and
    liquidized
pinch of grated nutmeg
salt and pepper
lemon wedges and cilantro leaves, to garnish

FILLING:
1 tbsp vegetable oil
3 scallions, thinly sliced
1 cup ricotta
4 tbsp natural yogurt
¾ cup Gruyère cheese, grated
1 egg, lightly beaten
1⅓ cups shelled shrimp, chopped
2 tbsp chopped parsley
pinch of cayenne pepper

1 Sift the flour and a pinch of salt into a bowl and tip in any bran remaining in the sifter. Beat together the egg, yogurt, water and oil. Gradually pour it onto the flour, beating all the time. Stir in the spinach purée and season with pepper and nutmeg.

2 To make the filling, heat the oil in a saucepan and fry the onions until translucent. Remove with a slotted spoon and drain on paper towels. Beat together the ricotta, yogurt, and half the Gruyère. Beat in the egg and stir in the shrimp and parsley. Season with salt and cayenne pepper.

3 Lightly brush a small, heavy skillet with oil and heat. Pour in 3-4 tablespoons of the pancake batter and tilt the pan so that it covers the base. Cook for about 3 minutes, until bubbles appear in the center. Turn and cook the other side for about 2 minutes, until lightly browned. Slide the pancake onto a warmed plate, cover with foil, and keep warm while you cook the remainder. It should make 8-12 pancakes.

4 Spread a little filling over each pancake and fold in half and then half again, envelope style. Spoon the remaining filling into the opening.

5 Grease a shallow ovenproof dish and arrange the pancakes in a single layer. Sprinkle on the remaining cheese and cook in the preheated oven for about 15 minutes. Serve hot, garnished with lemon and cilantro leaves.

CHAPTER FOUR

Meat & Poultry

Leg of lamb coated with an aromatic paste of yogurt, herbs and spices; rabbit flavored in a yogurt and herb marinade; tender cubes of lamb basted with yogurt and broiled until they are crisp on the outside, succulently pink inside; tandoori chicken baked in a spicy yogurt mixture which is served as a piquant sauce; moussaka baked until the yogurt and cheese custard topping is a sizzling toasty-brown – yogurt plays its part in meat dishes in so many ways.

Use it with olive oil, lemon juice, wine or vinegar in a marinade to tenderize the meat; use it in place of water or milk as a liquid element in pastry, and marvel at the difference it makes. And stir it into a sauce to complement meat meals from herb-flavored meatballs to casseroled pork. These and other dishes show that yogurt is not just a tasty added ingredient. It has a practical part to play in the preparation of a wide range of classic and country-style dishes.

Opposite: An idyllic rural scene in Tuscany, producer of much splendid meat and game. Yogurt marinades, coatings and toppings combine perfectly with meat and poultry dishes of all kinds.

STEP 1

STEP 3

STEP 4

STEP 5

CRISPY-COATED BABY CHICKEN

*You could adapt this recipe using a whole chicken or chicken pieces,
serving them on the bed of moist and colorful vegetables.*

SERVES 6
OVEN: 350°F

4 tbsp vegetable oil
1/4 cup butter
6 baby chicken, trussed
1 large onion, sliced
1 lb baby carrots
1 tbsp flour
2/3 cup white wine
juice of 2 oranges
2 fennel bulbs, quartered
1 1/4 cups chicken stock
1 tbsp green peppercorns, lightly crushed
1/2 tsp salt
1 tsp cornstarch
2/3 cup thick-set yogurt

COATING:
3 tbsp Turbinado or light brown sugar
1 tbsp green peppercorns, lightly crushed
3 tbsp coarse sea salt
2/3 cup thick-set yogurt

1 Heat the oil in a large skillet and add the butter. When bubbling, add the baby chicken in batches and brown evenly on all sides. Remove and keep warm.

2 Add the onion to the skillet and fry until translucent. Add the carrots,

stir to coat evenly, then sprinkle on the flour and blend well. Pour on the wine and orange juice, stirring all the time. Add the fennel, chicken stock, and peppercorns and season. Bring to the boil then pour into a roasting pan.

3 Arrange the baby chicken in the roasting pan, cover loosely with foil and cook in the preheated oven for 40 minutes.

4 To make the coating, stir together the sugar, peppercorns, salt, and yogurt to make a thick paste.

5 Preheat the broiler to high. Remove the baby chicken from the roasting pan and place them on a rack. Spread the paste evenly over the baby chickens, then broil for 3-4 minutes, until the coating is crisp.

6 Arrange the drained vegetables on a warm serving dish. Place the roasting pan over medium heat and bring the sauce to the boil. Stir the cornstarch into the yogurt, then blend into the sauce. Taste for seasoning. Place the baby chicken in the center of the dish, spoon a little sauce over the vegetables, and serve the rest separately.

LAMB KEBABS & CUCUMBER SAUCE

*Serve the kebabs sizzling hot and the sauce as cool as can be –
it is a delicious partnership.*

STEP 2

STEP 3

STEP 4

STEP 5

SERVES 4

2 lb lean leg of lamb, trimmed of fat
3 tbsp olive oil
1 tbsp red wine vinegar
juice of $^1/_2$ lemon
3 tbsp natural yogurt
1 tbsp dried oregano
2 large garlic cloves, crushed
2 dried bay leaves, crumbled
4 fresh bay leaves
2 tbsp chopped parsley
salt and pepper

SAUCE:
$1^1/_4$ cups natural yogurt
1 garlic clove, crushed
$^1/_4$ tsp salt
$^1/_2$ small cucumber, peeled and finely chopped
3 tbsp finely chopped mint
pinch of paprika

1 Cut the lamb into cubes about $1^1/_2$-2 in square. Pat dry with paper towels. This will help to ensure that the meat is crisp and firm on the outside when broiled.

2 Whisk together the olive oil, wine vinegar, lemon juice, and yogurt. Stir in the oregano, garlic, and crumbled bay leaves and season.

3 Place the meat cubes in the marinade and stir until well coated in the mixture. Cover and place in the refrigerator for at least 2 hours, for the meat to absorb the flavors.

4 Meanwhile, make the sauce. Place the yogurt in a large bowl. Stir in the garlic, salt, cucumber, and mint. Cover and set aside in the refrigerator. If it is more convenient, the sauce may be made several hours in advance.

5 Heat the broiler to high. With a slotted spoon, lift the meat from the marinade and shake off any excess liquid. Divide the meat into 4 equal portions. Thread the meat and the fresh bay leaves onto 4 skewers.

6 Broil the kebabs for about 4 minutes on each side, basting frequently with the marinade. At this stage the meat should be crisp on the outside and slightly pink on the inside. If you prefer it well done, cook the kebabs for a little longer.

7 Sprinkle the kebabs with parsley and serve at once with a tomato salad. Sprinkle the paprika over the sauce and serve chilled.

STEP 1

STEP 2

STEP 5

STEP 6

MOUSSAKA

*Both the meat sauce and the topping are lightly flavored
with cumin for a truly Greek taste.*

SERVES 6
OVEN: 375°F

1½ lb eggplant (about 2 small), thinly sliced
6 tbsp olive oil, plus extra for brushing
2 large onions, finely chopped
2 large garlic cloves, finely chopped
1½ lb lean ground lamb
2 tbsp tomato paste
½ tsp ground cumin
salt and pepper
5 tbsp chopped cilantro, or parsley

TOPPING:
4 eggs
2½ cups natural yogurt
½ tsp ground cumin
¼ cup feta cheese, crumbled
pepper
¼ cup Gruyère cheese, grated

1 Put the eggplant in a colander over a bowl and sprinkle with salt. Leave for about 1 hour, while the salt draws out the bitter juices, then rinse under cold, running water. Drain and pat dry with paper towels.

2 Heat 2 tablespoons of the oil in a skillet. Fry half the eggplant slices, turning them once, until evenly brown on both sides. Remove and keep warm. Heat another 2 tablespoons of the oil and fry the remaining slices in the same way. Remove and keep warm.

3 Add the remaining oil to the skillet and fry the onions until they are a light, golden brown. Stir in the chopped garlic. Add the meat and fry, stirring, until it changes color.

4 Stir in the tomato paste and cumin and season. Remove the pan from the heat and stir in the cilantro or parsley.

5 Brush a large ovenproof dish with olive oil. Arrange half the eggplant slices in the dish. Cover with the meat mixture, then arrange the remaining eggplant on top.

6 To make the topping, beat the eggs, then beat in the yogurt. Add the cumin and feta cheese, and season with pepper. Pour the sauce over the dish, and sprinkle on the grated cheese. Bake in the preheated oven for 45-50 minutes, until the top is dark golden brown and bubbling. Serve hot.

ORCHARD PORK

This is a quick and easy dish, ideal to serve to unexpected guests.

STEP 2

STEP 3

STEP 4

STEP 5

SERVES 4

1/4 cup butter
1 onion, chopped
1 garlic clove, finely chopped
1 lb pork tenderloin
1 tbsp paprika
2/3 cup chicken stock
1 1/4 cups natural yogurt
2 tsp cornstarch
2 apples
juice of 1/2 lemon
salt and pepper
parsley sprigs, to garnish
sautéed baby vegetables, to garnish (optional)

1 Heat half the butter in a skillet over a medium heat. Fry the onion until it is translucent. Then stir in the garlic and fry for 1 minute more.

2 Trim the pork of excess fat and cut into small thin slices. Pat the meat dry with paper towels. Add the pork to the skillet, sprinkle on the paprika and stir until the meat is coated with the spice. Cook for 3 minutes, stirring once or twice.

Pour in the chicken stock and stir well.
3 Bring to the boil, cover, and simmer for 10 minutes.
Mix together the yogurt and cornstarch to

4 make a smooth, thin paste. Stir it into the pork, season, and continue cooking for 10 minutes, stirring occasionally. Do not overheat or it will curdle.

Heat the remaining butter in a skillet.
5 Core and slice the apples and fry until they are golden brown on both sides.

Stir the lemon juice into the sauce and
6 taste to check the seasoning. Transfer the meat to a warmed serving dish, arrange the apple slices on top and garnish with parsley. Serve with baby vegetables, if liked.

MICROWAVE METHOD

Place half the butter in a dish and cook on high for 3 minutes. Stir in the pork and paprika, cover, and cook on high for 6 minutes. Add the stock, cover, and cook on high for 5 minutes. Stir in the yogurt, cornstarch and seasoning, cover, and cook on high for 4 minutes, stirring once. Remove the dish, stir, cover again, and stand for 5 minutes. Heat the remaining butter in a separate dish on high for 1 minute. Add the apples and cook on high for 3 minutes, stirring once.

STEP 1

STEP 2

STEP 4

STEP 5

HAM & CHICKEN PIE

Made with yogurt pastry, this pie has a really melt-in-the-mouth crust and a moist filling.

SERVES 6
OVEN: 400°F

2 cups flour, plus extra for dusting
1/2 tsp mustard powder
1/4 tsp salt
3/4 cup butter, cut into small pieces, plus
    extra for greasing
about 3 tbsp natural yogurt
2 tbsp milk
dill sprigs, to garnish

FILLING:
1/4 cup butter
1/4 cup flour
2/3 cup milk
2/3 cup natural yogurt
2 small leeks, sliced
1/2 lb boned, skinned chicken breast, diced
1 1/3 cups diced ham
1 tsp mushroom ketchup, or soy sauce
black pepper

1 Grease a pie pan 1¾ in deep. Sift together the flour, mustard powder, and salt and rub in the butter until the mixture resembles fine breadcrumbs. Stir in just enough yogurt to make a firm and non-sticky dough. Wrap in foil and chill.

2 Melt 2 tbsp of the butter in a small saucepan over a medium heat. Blend in the flour, then pour on the milk and yogurt, stirring all the time. Simmer, uncovered, for 5 minutes, then remove from the heat, transfer the sauce to a bowl and leave to cool.

3 Melt the remaining butter in a small saucepan and fry the leeks for 2-3 minutes, until they begin to soften.

4 Stir the leeks into the white sauce, add the chicken and ham, and cook for 3 minutes, until the chicken has changed color. Add the ketchup or soy sauce, and season, then leave to cool completely.

5 Roll out the pastry on a lightly floured board. Use just over half of it to line the prepared pan. Pour in the cold filling. Roll out the remaining pastry and cover the pie. Trim the edges and press them together. Brush the top with milk. Re-roll the pastry trimmings and cut into decorative shapes such as leaves or stars. Arrange the shapes over the pie and brush with milk. Bake the pie in the preheated oven for 35 minutes, or until the pastry is golden brown. Serve hot or cold.

TANDOORI CHICKEN

The yogurt and spices used to marinate the dish are served as a piquant sauce which may be poured over plain, boiled rice.

SERVES 4
OVEN: 400°F

²/₃ cup natural yogurt
¹/₂ tsp salt
1 tsp ground turmeric
1 tsp cumin seeds
1 tsp ground ginger
1 tsp garam masala (see page 78)
1 tsp chili powder, or to taste
3 garlic cloves, crushed
4 bay leaves, crumbled
2 tbsp tomato paste
juice of 2 limes, or 1 lemon
4 portions of chicken, about 12 oz each,
    skinned
¹/₂ cup Clarified Butter (see page 78)
2 tbsp paprika
Spiced Zucchini, to serve (see page 78)

STEP 3a

1 Put the yogurt in a bowl and stir in the salt, turmeric, cumin seeds, ginger, garam masala, and chili powder. Stir until well blended, then stir in the garlic, bay leaves, tomato paste, and lime or lemon juice.

2 Pour half the yogurt marinade into a shallow dish, spread evenly over the base and place the chicken pieces in a single layer on top. Spoon the remaining marinade over the chicken pieces to cover them completely. Loosely cover with foil and chill for at least 3 hours, or overnight. Spoon the marinade over the chicken from time to time.

3 Line a roasting pan with a piece of foil large enough to enclose it. Remove the chicken from the marinade and allow any excess to drain back into the bowl. Place the chicken pieces in the pan in a single layer. Pour the clarified butter over the chicken. Fold the foil over the pan and seal the edges so that no steam can escape.

4 Cook the chicken for 1 hour, then open the foil. Sprinkle the chicken evenly with paprika and return to the oven, uncovered, for a further 15 minutes.

5 Make the Spiced Zucchini (see page 78).

6 Transfer the chicken to a warmed serving dish with the Spiced Zucchini. Strain the marinade into a small saucepan, bring to the boil and boil rapidly for 2-3 minutes to reduce. Serve separately.

STEP 3b

STEP 5

SPICY MEATBALLS

*The creamy sauce is an ideal contrast to the spiciness of the meatballs,
and an unusual way of presenting beef.*

STEP 2

STEP 3

STEP 4

STEP 5

SERVES 4

4 tbsp olive oil
1 large onion, finely chopped
2 garlic cloves, finely chopped
1 lb lean ground beef
$^{3}/_{4}$ cup dry breadcrumbs
2 tbsp chopped cilantro or parsley
1 tsp cayenne pepper
3 tbsp natural yogurt
juice of $^{1}/_{2}$ lemon
salt and pepper
flour, for dusting
2 tbsp butter
noodles, to serve

SAUCE:
1 tbsp all-purpose flour
$^{3}/_{4}$ cup chicken stock
$^{2}/_{3}$ cup natural yogurt
1 tbsp chopped cilantro

1 Heat 2 tablespoons of the oil in a skillet and fry the onion until it is transparent. Add the garlic, and fry for 1 minute more. Set aside to cool.

2 Put the meat in a bowl and mash with a wooden spoon until it forms a sticky paste. Add the onion mixture, breadcrumbs, and cilantro or parsley. Stir in the paprika and cayenne pepper and mix well. Stir in the yogurt and lemon juice, season and stir until it forms a thick, sticky paste. Cover and chill for at least 30 minutes.

3 Flour your hands and shape the mixture into balls about the size of table-tennis balls. Roll each one in flour until evenly coated.

4 Heat the remaining oil and the butter in the skillet and fry the meatballs for 7-8 minutes, until they are firm and lightly colored on all sides. Remove with a slotted spoon.

5 To make the sauce, stir the flour into the remaining oil and fat. When well blended, gradually pour on the chicken stock, stirring constantly. Season and bring to the boil. Add the meatballs, cover and simmer over low heat for 30 minutes, turning the meatballs once or twice.

6 Stir in the yogurt, and taste for seasoning. Slowly reheat without bringing it to the boil. Remove from the heat and stir in half the cilantro. Transfer to a serving dish and sprinkle with remaining cilantro. Serve with buttered noodles.

ROAST LEG OF LAMB

*Prepare the lamb at least a day in advance and leave it in the
refrigerator so that the flavors can permeate the meat.*

STEP 1

SERVES 6
OVEN: 425°F;
THEN 350°F

1 x 1¹/₂-oz can anchovies, drained
4 lb leg of lamb
2 tbsp cilantro seeds
4 large garlic cloves, crushed
1¹/₄ cups natural yogurt
6-8 tbsp chopped parsley
1 bottle dry white wine
juice of 1 lemon
1 lb very small onions, peeled and left whole
3 tbsp butter
2 tbsp superfine sugar
²/₃ cup water
salt and pepper
fresh herbs, to garnish
new potatoes tossed in butter and parsley, to
 serve

1 Cut the anchovies in half and split
them lengthwise. Using a small,
sharp knife, make slits all over the lamb
and insert the anchovy pieces, folding if
necessary to push them in.

2 Lightly crush the cilantro seeds in a
pestle and mortar. Tip them into a
bowl, stir in the garlic, yogurt, and
parsley and season with pepper.

3 Spread the yogurt paste evenly
over the lamb, using the back of a
spoon to press it into the meat. Place the
lamb in a shallow dish, cover loosely
with foil, and leave in the refrigerator for
1-2 days, turning it once or twice.

4 Transfer the lamb to a roasting
pan. Pour in the wine and lemon
juice and cook uncovered for 15 minutes.
Lower the heat and continue roasting for
a further 1-1¼ hours, basting frequently.

5 Remove the meat from the oven,
cover with foil, and leave to rest in
a warm place for at least 15 minutes.
Pour the juices into a saucepan and boil
rapidly to reduce. Taste for seasoning.

6 Blanch the onions in boiling, salted
water for 3 minutes, then drain and
dry on paper towels. Melt the butter in a
pan and add the onions, sugar and
water. Simmer, uncovered, for 15
minutes, turning frequently. Watch
carefully towards the end, as the water
evaporates and the sugar caramelizes.

7 Transfer the meat to a serving dish
and spoon the onions around.
Serve with new potatoes and serve the
sauce separately.

STEP 3

STEP 5

STEP 6

STEP 2

STEP 3a

STEP 3b

STEP 4

RABBIT WITH FRIED CHEESE

*The topping is a simple but exquisite refinement to a country dish
of casseroled rabbit.*

SERVES 4
OVEN: 325°F

*2 lb rabbit pieces, washed and dried
salt
1 tbsp vegetable oil
3 tbsp butter
6 tbsp flour
1¼ cups chicken stock
2 tsp Dijon mustard
freshly ground black pepper
4 tbsp natural yogurt*

MARINADE:
*2 tbsp olive oil
1 small onion, sliced
²/₃ cup dry cider
2 tbsp white wine vinegar
2 sprigs each of rosemary and thyme
½ tsp juniper berries, crushed
½ tsp cilantro seeds, crushed
²/₃ cup natural yogurt*

TOPPING:
*1 cup yogurt cheese (see page 77), cut into
    4 slices
2 tbsp flour seasoned with 1 tsp dried thyme
    and freshly ground black pepper
3 tbsp olive oil*

1 Put all the marinade ingredients
except the yogurt in a small
saucepan. Bring to the boil, remove from
the heat, and allow to cool completely.

2 Beat the yogurt into the cold
marinade, and pour into a shallow
dish. Put the rabbit in the dish and spoon
over the marinade. Cover and chill for
several hours.

3 Heat the oil and butter in a
casserole. Drain the rabbit, then fry
until golden brown. Remove with a
slotted spoon and stir in the flour. Pour
the marinade into the casserole and
blend. Stir in the stock and mustard, and
season.

4 Return the rabbit to the casserole,
bring to the boil and cover. Cook in
the preheated oven for 1-1½ hours until
tender – test with a skewer. Strain the
sauce into a saucepan, stir in the yogurt,
and check the seasoning. Pour the sauce
over the rabbit.

5 To make the topping, toss the
yogurt cheese in the seasoned
flour. Heat the oil in a skillet and fry the
cheese for 2 minutes on each side, until
golden brown. Place the cheese on the
rabbit and serve, garnished with
rosemary.

CHAPTER FIVE

Desserts & Cakes

Yogurt's credentials as a tasty and delicious substitute for cream are never more convincing than in desserts and baked goods. By using cream and yogurt in equal proportions in crème brûlée, for example, you can retain the full dairy flavor with a significant reduction in fat and calorie content. By using yogurt in place of milk in a batter mixture you can introduce a surprising tanginess that contrasts well with the sweetness of fruit or an accompanying sauce, and by substituting natural yogurt for heavy cream in a luxurious cheesecake mixture you can serve a dinner party dessert that some guests might otherwise have considered over-rich.

Yogurt can be used to practical advantage, too, in traditional baking. Use it in place of buttermilk in light-as-a-feather biscuits and muffins, and in traditional gingerbread, where its blandness perfectly complements the rich combination of molasses, dark brown sugar, and dried fruits.

Opposite: Fresh fruit plus low-fat yogurt equals the perfect dessert – healthy and delicious.

STEP 2a

STEP 2b

STEP 3

STEP 4

APRICOT BRULEE

Serve this delicious dessert with caramelized meringues (see recipe below) for an extra-special occasion.

SERVES 6

²/₃ cup unsulphured apricots
²/₃ cup orange juice
4 egg yolks
2 tbsp superfine sugar
²/₃ cup yogurt
²/₃ cup heavy cream
1 tsp vanilla flavoring
¹/₂ cup Turbinado or light brown sugar
caramelized meringues to serve, optional

1 Soak the apricots in the orange juice for at least 1 hour. Pour into a small saucepan, bring slowly to the boil and simmer for 20 minutes. Purée in a blender or food processor.

2 Beat together the egg yolks and white sugar until the mixture is light and fluffy. Place the yogurt in a small saucepan, add the vanilla, and bring to the boil over a low heat. Pour the yogurt mixture over the eggs, beating all the time. Transfer to the top of a double boiler, or place the bowl over a pot of simmering water. Stir until the custard thickens.

3 Place the apricot mixture in 6 ramekins, and carefully pour on the custard. Cool, then leave to chill.

4 Heat the broiler to high. Sprinkle the turbinado sugar evenly over the custard and broil until the brown sugar caramelizes. Set aside to cool. To serve the brûlée, crack the hard caramel topping with the back of a tablespoon.

CARAMELIZED MERINGUES:
4 egg whites
6 tbsp superfine sugar
4 tbsp granulated sugar
¹/₄ cup blanched almonds, toasted

Whisk the egg whites until stiff. Whisk in the superfine sugar a little at a time, then whisk until the mixture is glossy and forms peaks. Pour water into a shallow skillet until ½ in deep and bring to simmering point. Take scoops of meringue, using 2 tablespoons, and place in the water. Poach for 2 minutes, turning them over once: do not allow the water to boil. Remove with a slotted spoon and place on baking parchment. For the caramel, place the granulated sugar in a small, heavy saucepan over a low heat. Shake the saucepan to distribute the sugar evenly, then leave it to caramelize, without stirring. Do not leave unattended. Transfer the meringues to a serving dish, pour on the caramel and scatter the almonds on top.

STEP 1

STEP 2

STEP 4

STEP 5

CHOCOLATE CHIP ICE CREAM

This frozen dessert offers the best of both worlds, delicious cookies and a rich dairy-flavored ice cream.

SERVES 6

1¼ cups milk
1 vanilla pod
2 eggs
2 egg yolks
¼ cup superfine sugar
1¼ cups natural yogurt
1⅓ cups Chocolate Chip Cookies, broken into
  small pieces (see page 77)

1 Pour the milk into a small saucepan, add the vanilla pod, and bring slowly to the boil. Remove from the heat, cover the pan, and leave to cool.

2 Beat the eggs and egg yolks in a double boiler, or in a bowl over a pot of simmering water. Add the sugar and continue beating until the mixture is pale and creamy.

3 Reheat the milk to simmering point and strain it over the egg mixture. Stir continuously until the custard is thick enough to coat the back of a spoon. Remove the custard from the heat and stand the pot or bowl in cold water to prevent any further cooking. Wash and dry the vanilla pod for future use. (See right for advice on using and storing vanilla pods.)

4 Stir the yogurt into the cooled custard and beat until it is well blended. When the mixture is thoroughly cold, stir in the broken cookies.

5 Transfer the mixture to a chilled metal cake pan or plastic container, cover and freeze for 4 hours. Remove from the freezer every hour, transfer to a chilled bowl and beat vigorously to prevent ice crystals forming. Alternatively, freeze the mixture in an ice cream maker, following the manufacturer's instructions.

6 To serve the ice cream, transfer it to the main part of the refrigerator for 1 hour. Serve in scoops.

VANILLA PODS

Vanilla pods can be used to flavor any hot liquid. For a stronger flavor, split the pod lengthwise with a sharp knife before infusing it in the hot liquid for 20-30 minutes. For a very strong flavor, scrape the seeds out of the pod and add to the liquid when infusing. Rinse and dry the pod after use. It can be stored in a jar of sugar, to which it will impart its flavor.

PASHKA

A Russian dessert traditionally served at Easter, this dish is begun at least 24 hours before serving.

SERVES 8

3½ *cups natural yogurt*
2 *eggs*
½ *cup superfine sugar*
⅔ *cup sweet butter, softened*
⅔ *cup heavy cream*
⅓ *cup candied orange peel, chopped*
⅓ *cup dried apricots, chopped*
½ *cup seedless raisins*
¾ *cup blanched almonds, chopped*
1 *tsp orange-flower water*

TO DECORATE:

A selection of candied stalks and fruits, such as angelica, pineapple, greengages, pears and glacé cherries

1 Begin by making the yogurt cheese. Tip the yogurt into a colander lined with muslin or cheesecloth. Draw up the ends, tie firmly and hang up the bag to drain overnight.

2 Turn the drained yogurt cheese into a large bowl. Beat together the eggs and sugar until they are light and fluffy, then gradually beat the mixture into the yogurt cheese. Beat in the butter, then stir in the heavy cream.

3 Stir the candied peel, apricots, raisins, and almonds into the cheese mixture, then sprinkle on the orange-flower water and stir it in.

4 Thoroughly wash and dry a flower-pot and line it with 2 layers of muslin or cheesecloth. Spoon the mixture into the pot and fold over the ends of the cloth to enclose it. Stand the pot in a dish and place a small plate on top so that it fits just inside the rim. Place a heavy weight or some food cans on top and place the pot in the refrigerator for at least 12 hours.

5 To turn out the dessert, unfold the cheesecloth, place a serving dish over the top of the container and invert it. When the dessert has been released, carefully ease away the cloth.

6 Decorate the top and sides of the dessert with slices of candied fruits arranged in a pattern. The bright green angelica can be used to represent leaves or stalks. Serve the dessert chilled, cut into wedge-shaped slices.

STEP 2

STEP 3

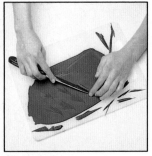

STEP 5a

STEP 5b

BOSTON CHOCOLATE PIE

*A lighter version of the popular chocolate cream pie,
this dessert is made with yogurt pastry.*

SERVES 6
OVEN: 400°F

$^1/_2$ lb Yogurt Pastry (see page 44), but omit
    the mustard powder

FILLING:
3 eggs
$^1/_2$ cup superfine sugar
$^1/_2$ cup flour, plus extra for dusting
1 tbsp confectioners' sugar
pinch of salt
1 tsp vanilla flavoring
1$^3/_4$ cups milk
$^2/_3$ cup natural yogurt
*5 squares bittersweet chocolate, broken into
    pieces*
2 tbsp kirsch

TOPPING:
$^2/_3$ cup crème fraîche
Chocolate Caraque (see page 77)

1 Grease a 9-in pie pan. Roll out the
pastry on a lightly floured board
and lower into the pan. Press into the
pan and around the sides and roll the
rolling pin over the top to trim it neatly.
Prick the base with a fork, line with
parchment paper and fill it with dried
beans. Bake for 20 minutes, then remove

the beans and paper and return to the
oven for 5 minutes to dry. Remove from
the oven and leave on a wire rack to cool.

2 To make the filling, beat the eggs
and sugar until light and fluffy. Put
the flour, confectioners' sugar, and salt in
a sieve, sift over the beaten eggs and stir
until thoroughly blended. Stir in the
vanilla flavoring.

3 Put the milk and yogurt in a small
saucepan, bring slowly to the boil,
then strain onto the egg mixture. Pour
into the top of a double boiler, or a bowl
over a saucepan of simmering water, and
stir until thick enough to coat the back of
a spoon.

4 Put the chocolate and kirsch into a
small saucepan over a low heat.
When it has melted, stir into the custard.
Remove the custard from the heat and
stand the double boiler or bowl in cold
water to prevent further cooking. Leave
it to cool .

5 Make the Chocolate Caraque (see
page 77). Pour the chocolate
mixture into the pastry case. Spread the
crème fraîche over the chocolate, and
arrange the caraque rolls on top.

STEP 1

STEP 2

STEP 3

STEP 4

CHERRY CLAFOUTIS

A sweet batter pudding that has its origins in both England and France;
it may be eaten straight from the oven, or slightly warm.

SERVES 4-6
OVEN: 375°F

3 eggs
3 tbsp flour
pinch of salt
½ tbsp ground cinnamon
4 tbsp superfine sugar, plus extra for
  sprinkling
1¼ cups milk
⅔ cup natural yogurt
2 tbsp dark rum (optional)
1½ lb black cherries, stalks removed, and
  pitted (about 4½ cups)
1 tbsp butter, plus extra for greasing

1 Grease a shallow, ovenproof dish. Lightly beat the eggs in a bowl. Put the flour, salt, cinnamon and sugar in a sieve, sift the dry ingredients over the eggs and beat the mixture until it is pale and creamy.

2 Pour the milk, yogurt, and rum into a small saucepan and heat to simmering point. Pour over the egg mixture and beat thoroughly.

3 Place the cherries in the base of the prepared dish and spoon the batter over them. Dot the butter over the top of the pudding.

4 Bake in the preheated oven for 30 minutes, or until well risen and golden brown on top. To test, insert a fine skewer into the center: it should come out clean. Sprinkle with superfine sugar, and serve hot or warm.

VARIATION

Clafoutis limousin is a traditional French batter dessert (they leave the stones in the cherries). Make in the same way, let cool until just warm – it will sink slightly – then sprinkle with 2-3 tablespoons of Armagnac and a little confectioners' sugar.

STEP 1

STEP 2

STEP 3

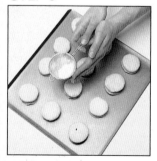

STEP 4

YOGURT MUFFINS

Yogurt is a suitable alternative to buttermilk, providing just the acidity needed to produce perfect scones. This basic recipe can be varied in many ways.

MAKES ABOUT 16
OVEN: 450°F

2 cups flour, plus extra for dusting
1 tsp salt
1 tbsp baking powder
¹/₄ cup sweet butter, chilled, plus extra for greasing
1¹/₂ tbsp sugar
1 egg
6 tbsp natural yogurt

1 Sift together the flour, salt, and baking powder. Cut the butter into small pieces, and rub it into the dry ingredients until the mixture resembles dry breadcrumbs. Stir in the sugar.

2 Beat together the egg and yogurt and stir it quickly into the dry ingredients. Mix to form a thick dough and knead until it is smooth and free from cracks.

3 Lightly flour a pastry board and rolling pin and roll out the dough to a thickness of ¾ in. Cut out circles with a 2-in pastry cutter, gather up the trimmings and roll them out again. Cut out as many more circles as possible.

4 Grease a baking sheet lightly with butter and heat it in the oven. Transfer the dough circles to the sheet and dust lightly with flour.

5 Bake the muffins in the oven for 10 minutes, or until they are well risen and golden brown. Transfer them to a wire rack to cool. Serve warm, with honey or jam and with butter and whipped cream.

VARIATIONS

You can vary the recipe to make a selection of biscuits and muffins:
For spiced muffins, sift up to 1½ teaspoons ground ginger or cinnamon with the flour and other dry ingredients.
For dried fruit, seed or nut muffins, stir in up to ½ cup raisins, currants, chopped dried apricots, dates or figs; up to 2 tablespoons sunflower seeds, or up to ½ cup chopped walnuts, hazelnuts, almonds, or pecans. These ingredients should be stirred in with the sugar at the end of step 1.
For biscuits, omit the sugar in the recipe. At the end of step 1, stir in up to ⅓ cup grated Cheddar or other hard cheese; up to 2 teaspoons dried herbs, such as oregano or thyme or up to 5 teaspoons fresh chopped herbs.

STEP 1

STEP 3a

STEP 3b

STEP 5

TRUFFLE CHEESECAKE

The combination of flavors that are built up through the layers, from almond through coffee to chocolate, make this dessert a memorable experience.

Serves 8
Oven: 400°F;
then 275°F

¹/₄ cup sweet butter
1¹/₂ cups Amaretti cookies, crushed
1 cup yogurt cheese (see page 77) or
    low-fat soft cheese
1 cup mascarpone
²/₃ cup crème fraîche
¹/₂ tsp vanilla flavoring
6 tbsp superfine sugar
2 eggs, plus 1 egg yolk
1 tbsp flour
1 tbsp instant coffee granules
¹/₂ cup boiling water
2 tbsp coffee liqueur, or brandy
7 ladyfingers

Topping:
1 tbsp sweet butter
²/₃ cup natural yogurt
¹/₄ cup superfine sugar
5 squares bittersweet chocolate, broken up
1 tbsp coffee liqueur or brandy
1 tbsp cocoa powder

1 Grease and line a 7-in spring-form pan. Melt the butter in a small saucepan over low heat. Remove from the heat, stir in the crumbs and tip them into the prepared pan. Press the crumbs to cover the base evenly and chill.

2 Beat together the yogurt cheese, mascarpone, crème fraîche, and vanilla. Beat in the sugar, eggs, egg yolk, and flour. Pour half into the pan.

3 Dissolve the coffee in the boiling water, add the liqueur, and pour into a small bowl. Quickly dip the sponge biscuits in the coffee. Arrange the ladyfingers over the cheese mixture and spoon on the remainder.

4 Bake in the preheated oven for 20 minutes, then lower the heat and cook for a further 1½ hours, or until a fine skewer inserted in the center comes out clean. Allow the cake to cool completely before removing it from the pan.

5 Bring the butter, yogurt, and sugar to the boil. Add the chocolate and liqueur and stir over a low heat for 2-3 minutes. Remove from the heat and beat to blend thoroughly. Leave until completely cold, then spoon the mixture into a pastry bag and pipe lines or squiggles over the top of the cheesecake. Just before serving, dust the top with cocoa powder.

DANISH LEMON CAKE

Cardamom seeds, the familiar flavoring of Danish pastries, contribute a subtle spiciness to this light sandwich cake.

STEP 2

SERVES 6-8
OVEN: 375°F

³/₄ cup butter or margarine, softened, plus extra for greasing
³/₄ cup superfine sugar
3 eggs
1¹/₂ cups self-rising flour, sifted, plus extra for dusting
2 tsp grated lemon rind
1 tbsp lemon juice
2 tbsp natural yogurt
8 cardamom pods

FILLING:
4 tbsp natural yogurt
4 tbsp confectioners' sugar, sifted, plus extra for dusting
4 tbsp lemon curd

1 Grease 2 x 7-in diameter shallow cake pans and dust them with flour. In a bowl beat together the butter or margarine and the sugar until the mixture is pale and golden. Beat in the eggs one at a time, beating in a tablespoon of the sifted flour after each addition to prevent the mixture from curdling. Fold in the remaining flour with a metal spoon, then stir in the lemon rind, lemon juice and yogurt.

STEP 3

2 Split the cardamom pods with a small, sharp knife. Remove the hard, black seeds and crush them with a pestle and mortar, or tap them lightly with a small hammer. Discard the pods and stir the crushed seeds into the cake mixture.

3 Divide the mixture between the 2 prepared pans and level the surface. Bake in the oven for 25 minutes, until the cakes are well risen and feel springy to the touch. Stand the pans on a wire rack to cool, then turn the cakes out to cool completely.

STEP 4

4 To make the filling, mix together the yogurt and confectioners' sugar, then beat in the lemon curd. Beat in a little more sifted sugar if necessary, to make a stiff, spreadable consistency.

5 Sandwich the 2 halves of the cake with the filling, and dust the top with sifted confectioners' sugar.

STEP 5

STEP 1

STEP 2

STEP 3

STEP 4

SCOTTISH GINGERBREAD

*This dark brown, spicy cake should be made well in advance of serving.
It is best kept for at least 2 weeks, closely wrapped in foil.*

SERVES 8
OVEN: 350°F

1¼ cups wholewheat flour
½ tsp salt
2 tsp ground ginger
1 tsp ground cinnamon
grated nutmeg
2 tsp baking powder
1 cup dark brown moist sugar
1⅓ cups rolled oats
6 tbsp molasses (see below)
½ cup butter
1 egg, beaten
⅔ cup natural yogurt
¾ cup raisins
scant 1 cup crystalized ginger, chopped
½ cup blanched almond halves
⅔ cup milk

1 Grease and line a 7-in round cake pan. Sift the flour, salt, ground ginger, cinnamon, nutmeg, and baking powder into a bowl and tip in any bran remaining in the sifter. Stir in the sugar and rolled oats.

2 Put the molasses and butter into a small saucepan and warm it over low heat. Remove from the heat and stir with a wooden spoon to blend thoroughly.

3 Stir the butter mixture into the dry ingredients, then beat in the egg and yogurt. Stir in the raisins and crystalized ginger. Stir in just enough milk to give a stiff, dropping consistency.

4 Spoon the mixture into the prepared pan and level the surface. Arrange the nuts over the surface. Bake in the preheated oven for 1½ hours, or until a fine skewer inserted in the center of the cake comes out clean.

5 Leave the cake to cool in the pan, then turn it out and stand on a wire rack to cool completely. Wrap closely in foil to store. Serve sliced, with yogurt cheese and honey, or with well-matured hard cheese and fresh fruit such as apples and pears.

MOLASSES TREACLE

An easy way to measure molasses is to dip 2 tablespoons into boiling water until they are hot. Use one spoon to scoop out the molasses and the other to push it into the saucepan. Reheat the spoons as often as necessary.

STEP 1

STEP 3

STEP 4

STEP 5

PASSION CAKE

Decorating this moist, rich carrot cake with sugared flowers lifts it into the celebration class. It is a perfect choice for Easter.

SERVES 8-10
OVEN: 350°F

$2/3$ cup corn oil
$3/4$ cup superfine sugar
4 tbsp natural yogurt
3 eggs, plus 1 extra yolk
1 tsp vanilla flavoring
1 cup walnut pieces, chopped
1 cup shredded carrots
1 banana, mashed
$1^1/2$ cups flour
$1/2$ cup fine oatmeal
1 tsp baking soda
1 tsp baking powder
1 tsp ground cinnamon
$1/2$ tsp salt

FROSTING:
generous $1/2$ cup yogurt cheese (see page 77), or low-fat soft cheese
4 tbsp natural yogurt
$3/4$ cup confectioners' sugar
1 tsp grated lemon rind
2 tsp lemon juice

DECORATION:
a few primroses and violets
3 tbsp superfine sugar
1 egg white, lightly beaten

1 Grease and line a 9-in round cake pan. Beat together the oil, sugar, yogurt, eggs, egg yolk, and vanilla flavoring. Beat in the chopped walnuts, shredded carrots and banana.

2 Sift together the remaining ingredients and gradually beat into the mixture.

3 Pour the mixture into the pan and level the surface. Bake in the preheated oven for $1\frac{1}{2}$ hours, or until the cake is firm. To test, insert a fine skewer into the center: it should come out clean. Leave to cool in the pan for 15 minutes, then turn out on a wire rack.

4 To make the frosting, beat together the cheese and yogurt. Sift in the confectioners' sugar and stir in the lemon rind and juice. Spread over the top and sides of the cake.

5 To prepare the decoration, dip the flowers quickly in the beaten egg white, then sprinkle with superfine sugar to cover the surface completely. Place well apart on parchment paper. Leave in a warm, dry place for several hours until they are dry and crisp. Arrange the flowers in a pattern on top of the cake.

WHAT IS YOGURT?

NEW POTATO SALAD

Serves 4

1 lb small new potatoes, scrubbed
salt
2 scallions thinly sliced
1 egg, hard-boiled and chopped

Dressing:

2 tbsp natural yogurt
2 tbsp olive oil
1 tbsp red wine vinegar
large pinch of mustard powder
pepper

1. Cook the potatoes in boiling, salted water until they are just tender, then drain.

2. To make the dressing, beat together the yogurt, oil, vinegar, and mustard powder and season with salt and pepper.

3. Pour the dressing over the potatoes while they are still hot and toss thoroughly. Set aside to cool.

4. Stir the scallions into the potato salad, transfer to a serving dish and garnish with chopped hard-boiled egg.

No one knows who first invented yogurt, or where in the world it was first recognized as a healthy way of keeping fresh milk beyond its normal use-by date. It seems probable that it was discovered by nomadic tribesmen crossing the vast Asian continent, carrying fresh milk from one camp to the next in primitive bags made from the lining of sheep's stomachs. Exposed to the heat of the sun and not sterilized in any way, these containers would have provided ideal nursery conditions for the still-present bacteria to grow.

Speculating again, it was probably only a short step from the nomads' first taste of this not-quite-sweet, not-quite-sour dairy food to the discovery that a little of yesterday's yogurt added to today's milk will become tomorrow's fresh batch of yogurt.

A taste for yogurt spread far beyond its original homelands, and down the centuries many claims have been made for its beneficial properties, not least that it is "the milk of eternal life".

In our own time yogurt is enjoyed for its versatility and convenience. A tub of yogurt in the refrigerator has the makings of an instant snack or dessert; a hasty sauce, salad dressing or dip; a tenderizing marinade or coating and, as our recipes show, a significant ingredient in dishes of all kinds.

More than that, yogurt offers the consistency of a dairy product such as cream or crème fraîche, with a much lower fat content.

MAKING YOGURT

Although there is only one basic way of making yogurt - by stirring hot milk into a prepared yogurt culture or a spoonful of starter from a previous batch - there is enough scope for variation to satisfy the most experimental cook. You can use any combination of any kind of milk from cows, goats or sheep, skimmed or semi-skimmed, sterilized, homogenized, pasteurized, or evaporated. For a luxurious-tasting result you can make yogurt with a proportion of light cream and milk, and for a thicker product you can stir 1 tablespoon of powdered milk into whatever milk you use.

Yogurt culture is made with either *Lactobacillus bulgaricus* or *Lactobacillus acidopholus*, which develop most readily when the milk is added at a temperature between 90° and 120°F and is allowed to cool to a constant temperature no lower than 65°F for the 8 hours it takes the yogurt to set.

Primitive and non-scientific methods of achieving this included putting the maturing yogurt in a covered container inside a "hay box" cooker, or in a specially padded and insulated pan, on a tray in the oven. If you want to eliminate the element of chance, you can use an electric yogurt-maker, which is thermostatically controlled to keep the developing culture at the correct temperature.

YOGURT

MAKES 4 CUPS

4 cups milk
1 tbsp natural yogurt, or a package of
* commercial culture*

1. Pour the milk into a saucepan and, unless it has already been sterilized, bring it to the boil, then turn off the heat. Allow it to cool until, when you dip in a clean finger, you can keep it in the milk without discomfort while you count slowly to 10. If the milk is sterilized you need only heat it to 90°-120°F.

2. Put the starter yogurt in a small bowl, pour on a little of the milk and beat it thoroughly.

3. Pour the yogurt mixture into the milk remaining in the saucepan and stir to blend it thoroughly.

4. Pour the milk mixture into a scrupulously clean container such as an earthenware or heatproof glass bowl, a number of small containers or a yogurt maker.

5. Cover the containers and set aside in a warm place, without disturbing them, for 8-10 hours. The longer you leave the culture in the warmth, the more acidic it will become and the more the flavor will sharpen.

6. Transfer the yogurt to the refrigerator, and remember to save at least 1 tablespoon to start the next batch.

Storing yogurt

Yogurt continues to change its character even in the chill temperature of a refrigerator. You can store it, in a covered container, for up to seven days, but by then it may start to separate and will have developed a sharp, tangy flavor. It is best to use some to make your next batch of yogurt before it reaches that stage. Homemade yogurt does not freeze satisfactorily, and frozen yogurt cannot be used as a starter.

Stabilizing yogurt

If you plan to use yogurt in a recipe which involves adding cold yogurt to a hot liquid, or in which the yogurt will be brought to boiling point, it is best to stabilize it first, to prevent separation. The way to do this, using cornstarch to thicken it, is described on page 12. Although separation will not affect the flavor of the dish, it does spoil the texture and appearance.

Do not use stabilized yogurt as a starter to make another batch. The high temperature at which it is stirred will kill the bacteria.

YOGURT CHEESE

Once you are in the habit of making your own yogurt, or if you buy yogurt in reasonably large quantities, the next step is to make your own soft cheese. You can use it in place of cottage cheese or commercially made low-fat soft cheese in a wide variety of dishes.

The yield varies slightly according to the type of milk from which the yogurt was made, and the length of time it was

CHOCOLATE CHIP COOKIES

MAKES ABOUT 26
OVEN: 375°F

6 tbsp sweet butter, softened
¼ cup superfine sugar
½ cup moist light brown sugar
1 egg, lightly beaten
1 ½ cups self-rising flour
pinch of salt
½ tsp vanilla flavoring
3 squares bittersweet chocolate,
* chopped*

1. Brush 2 baking sheets with vegetable oil. Beat the butter and sugar until the mixture is thick and creamy. Beat in the egg, then stir in the flour, salt, vanilla, and chocolate pieces.

2. Drop teaspoon-sized heaps of the mixture well apart on to the prepared baking sheets. Bake in the preheated oven for 12-15 minutes until the cookies are golden brown. Transfer to a wire rack to cool, then store in an airtight container.

CHOCOLATE CARAQUE
Spread the chocolate pieces on a large plate over a saucepan of simmering water until melted, then use a palette knife to spread it on a cool surface. When cool, scrape it into curls by drawing a sharp knife blade firmly across the surface.

SPICED ZUCCHINI

4 tbsp vegetable oil
3 medium zucchini, sliced
1 cup natural yogurt
2 garlic cloves, crushed
*1/2 tsp cumin seeds, lightly
    crushed*
pinch of chili powder
large pinch of paprika
salt

1. Heat the oil in a skillet and fry the zucchini, in a single layer, until light brown on all sides. Transfer to a warmed dish.

2. Place the yogurt in a bowl, stir in the garlic, cumin seeds and chili powder and season. Just before serving, pour over the zucchini and sprinkle with paprika.

CLARIFIED BUTTER
To clarify butter, place 1/2 cup sweet butter in a small saucepan. Melt the butter over low heat, then strain into a bowl. Discard the sediment that collects at the base of the saucepan.

GARAM MASALA
This sweet, gentle mixture of spices used in Indian cooking may be found in supermarkets and specialty stores.

left to drain. As a guide, any quantity of yogurt will provide just over half its volume in yogurt cheese. The whey that is drained off can be stored in the refrigerator and used in place of stock in soups and sauces.

TO MAKE 1½ CUPS CHEESE

4 cups natural yogurt
salt (optional)

1. Line a colander with a double thickness of cheesecloth or muslin. Tip in the yogurt and draw the muslin over to cover it. Or tie the corners of the muslin to make a bag. Stand the colander in a bowl, or hang the bag over a bowl, to catch the whey.

2. Leave it to drain overnight. Transfer the yogurt to a bowl and, if you wish, beat in a little salt. Store in a covered container in the refrigerator for up to a week.

Storing yogurt cheese
You may like to store some of your yogurt cheese in the traditional Middle Eastern way. Scoop out small spoonfuls and roll them into walnut-sized balls. Pack them in a lidded jar and pour on olive oil to cover the cheese completely. Add any flavorings you wish, such as bay leaves, sprigs of thyme or rosemary, dried chilies, peppercorns or mustard seeds.

To serve, lift out the cheese as required with a draining spoon, drain off the excess oil, and roll the balls in chopped walnuts. Serve these cheese balls as an appetizer with drinks.

YOGURT DRINKS

Sweet or salty, chilled and tingling with ice, yogurt drinks are deeply rooted in Middle Eastern and Indian cuisines. And now, increasingly, their popularity is spreading as more of us wake up to the news that a long, cool glass of yogurt-plus is as refreshing and revitalizing as an early morning cup of coffee.

You can make a pitcher of Ayran or Lassi overnight and chill it to serve in an instant in the morning; serve it before a spicy meal to prepare the palate for the medley of flavors to come, or as an accompaniment to an Indian meal, when the contrast of bland and spicy, hot and cold elements will be specially pleasing.

You can also add your own combination of fruits and syrups, cereals and nuts until you have a nutritious meal in a glass; just the thing for anyone who takes breakfast at the double, or for serving to children who refuse a "proper" breakfast.

AYRAN

This is the favorite soft drink in Turkey and other Middle Eastern countries, where it is sold, refreshingly chilled, by street sellers.

SERVES 2
1¼ cups natural yogurt, chilled
1¼ cups water, chilled
½ tsp salt
*½ tsp dried mint, or 1 tsp chopped fresh
    mint*
ice cubes, to serve
mint sprigs, to garnish (optional)

Whisk together the yogurt and water and stir in the salt and mint. Store in a covered container in the refrigerator if it is not to be served at once.

To serve, add ice cubes and, if you wish, a sprig of mint, and serve in chilled glasses, with straws.

LASSI

Some Indian restaurant menus offer a salt drink similar to Ayran, or a sweet version, which may include any combination of nuts, chopped dried fruits, shredded coconut and food coloring.

SERVES 2

*1¼ cups natural yogurt, chilled
1¼ cups milk, chilled
1 tsp rosewater or orange-flower water
2 tsp shredded coconut
1 tbsp seedless raisins
2 tsp superfine sugar
ice cubes, to serve
ground cinnamon, to sprinkle (optional)*

Whisk together the yogurt, milk, and rosewater or orange-flower water and stir in the coconut, raisins, and sugar. Pour into two tall, chilled glasses, add the ice cubes and, if you wish, sprinkle a little ground cinnamon on top. Serve chilled, with straws and long-handled spoons.

BANANA COOLER

This "meal-in-a-glass" is especially good at breakfast.

SERVES 2

*1¼ cups natural yogurt, chilled
1 tbsp honey
2 small bananas, chopped
1 tbsp muesli
ground cinnamon, to sprinkle (optional)*

Put the yogurt, honey, and bananas into a blender or food processor, and process until smooth. Divide the mixture between 2 glasses and sprinkle each one with muesli and, if you wish, ground cinnamon. Serve with straws and long-handled spoons.

FRUIT WHIP

A frothy yogurt version of a milkshake, this drink seems appropriate to long, lazy afternoons in summer.

SERVES 4

*1¼ cups natural yogurt, chilled
1¼ cups fruit purée, such as strawberry raspberry, apple, or dried apricot, chilled
1 tbsp honey
1 egg white, stiffly beaten
fresh fruit or herbs, to decorate*

Whisk together the yogurt, fruit purée, and honey. Fold in the egg white and divide between 4 glasses. Decorate with fruit or herbs. Serve with straws.

FLAVORING YOGURT
Whether you make your own yogurt or buy large cartons of natural yogurt in the supermarket, it is rewarding to have your own repertoire of flavorings, which will soon become family favorites.

Sweet flavorings
- Crumbled chocolate flake and chopped hazelnuts
- Fresh strawberries and strawberry syrup
- Chopped orange segments with concentrated orange juice and grated orange rind
- Chopped Turkish delight and a sprinkling of rosewater
- Honey and a few pomegranate seeds
- Chopped dates and blanched almonds
- Chopped stewed dried apricots and apricot brandy

Savory Blends
These blends can be served as sauces and as appetizing dips, with potato chips, crackers or crudités:

- Chopped watercress and chopped macadamia nuts, with a dash of lemon juice
- Mayonnaise, chopped hard-boiled egg, and snipped chives
- Mayonnaise, capers, chopped green pepper, and snipped scallion tops
- Lumpfish roe, lemon juice and chopped parsley
- Grated horseradish, heavy cream, and chopped mint

INDEX

Almonds: pashka, 61
Amaretti cookies: truffle cheesecake, 68
anchovies: roast leg of lamb, 51
apples: orchard pork, 42
apricots: apricot brulée, 56
  pashka, 61
artichoke mousse, 9
avocados: poached salmon, 16
ayran, 78-9

Banana cooler, 79
batter: cherry clafoutis, 64
beef: spicy meatballs, 48
bell pepper salad, 9
Boston chocolate pie, 62
brulée, apricot, 56
butter, clarified, 78

Cakes: Danish lemon cake, 71
  passion cake, 74
  Scottish gingerbread, 72
candied orange peel: pashka, 61
caramel: apricot brulée, 56
caraque, chocolate, 77
cardamom: Danish lemon cake, 71
carrots: crispy-coated baby chicken, 36
  passion cake, 74
cauliflower roulade, 28
cheese, 77-8
  baked red snapper, 20
  cauliflower roulade, 28
  moussaka, 40
  rabbit with fried cheese, 52
  savoury muffins, 66
  smoked salmon cheesecake, 10
  spinach pancakes, 32
  truffle cheesecake, 68
cheesecakes: smoked salmon, 10
  truffle, 68
cherry clafoutis, 64
chicken: baby, crispy-coated, 36
  ham and chicken pie, 44
  tandoori chicken, 47
chocolate: Boston chocolate pie, 62
  chocolate caraque, 77
  chocolate chip cookies, 77
  chocolate chip ice-cream, 58
  truffle cheesecake, 68
chowder, fish and seafood, 22
clafoutis: cherry clafoutis, 64
  clafoutis limousin, 64
clarified butter, 78
coffee: truffle cheesecake, 68

cookies, chocolate chip, 77
corn: fish and seafood chowder, 22
cream: apricot brulée, 56
  pashka, 61
crème fraîche: truffle cheesecake, 68
cucumber: lamb kebabs and cucumber
  sauce, 38
curries: shrimp curry and fruit sauce,
  25

Danish lemon cake, 71
desserts, 55-65, 68
dried fruit muffins, 66
drinks, 78-9

Eggplant: moussaka, 40

First courses, 7-12
fish, 15-25
  baked red snapper, 20
  fish and seafood chowder, 22
  poached salmon, 16
  quenelles and watercress sauce, 18
  smoked salmon cheesecake, 10
flavoring yogurt, 79
fruit sauce, 25
fruit whip, 79

Gingerbread, Scottish, 72

Haddock, smoked see smoked
  haddock
ham and chicken pie, 44

Ice cream, chocolate chip, 58

Kebabs: lamb, and cucumber sauce,
  38

Lamb: lamb kebabs and cucumber
  sauce, 38
  moussaka, 40
  roast leg of lamb, 51
lassi, 79
lemon cake, Danish, 71

Meat and poultry, 35-52
meatballs, spicy, 48
milk: lassi, 79
  making yogurt, 76-7
mint: ayran, 78-9
  lamb kebabs and cucumber sauce,
  38
molasses: measuring, 72
  Scottish gingerbread, 72

moussaka, 40
mousse, artichoke, 9
muffins: dried fruit, seed or nut, 66
  savoury, 66
  spiced, 66
  yogurt, 66
mussels: fish and seafood chowder, 22

Oatmeal: Scottish gingerbread, 72
onions: roast leg of lamb, 51
orchard pork, 42

Pancakes, spinach, 32
pashka, 61
passion cake, 74
pepper salad, 9
pies: Boston chocolate pie, 62
  ham and chicken pie, 44
pitas: vegetable medley, 31
pork, orchard, 42
potatoes: fish and seafood chowder, 22
  new potato salad, 76
poultry and meat, 35-52
shrimp: shrimp curry and fruit sauce,
  25
  spinach pancakes, 32

Quenelles and watercress sauce, 18

Rabbit with fried cheese, 52
raisins: fruit sauce, 25
  pashka, 61
red snapper, baked, 20
roulade, cauliflower, 28

Salads: bell pepper, 9
  new potato, 76
salmon, poached, 16
  see also smoked salmon
sauces: cucumber, 38
  fruit, 25
  watercress, 18
savoury biscuits, 66
scallions : spinach pancakes, 32
Scottish gingerbread, 72
seafood: fish and seafood chowder, 22
shrimp : shrimp curry and fruit
  sauce, 25
  spinach pancakes, 32
smoked haddock: fish and seafood
  chowder, 22
smoked salmon cheesecake, 10
soups: fish and seafood chowder, 22
  yogurt and spinach, 12
spiced muffins, 66

spicy meatballs, 48
spinach: spinach pancakes, 32
  yogurt and spinach soup, 12
scallions: spinach pancakes, 32
stabilizing yogurt, 12, 77
storing yogurt, 77
storing yogurt cheese, 78

Tandoori chicken, 47
tomatoes: baked red snapper, 20
truffle cheesecake, 68

Vanilla pods, 58
vegetables, 27-32
  vegetable medley, 31

Walnuts: passion cake, 74
watercress: cauliflower roulade, 28
  quenelles and watercress sauce, 18

Yogurt, 76-9
  making, 76-7
yogurt cheese, 77-8
  baked red snapper, 20
  cauliflower roulade, 28
  passion cake, 74
  rabbit with fried cheese, 52
  truffle cheesecake, 68

Zucchini, spiced, 78